Potholders

and other
loopy
projects

Barbara Kane

KLUTZ®

Contents

hook

needle

loops

What you get

loom

yarn

Weaving 101

To learn to weave, it helps to know two words:

WARP
The loops (or yarn) stretched on the loom before weaving

warp loops

weft loop

WEFT
The loops woven over and under the warp loops

warp loops

Weaving Workshop

1 Pick out colors for your first square — 18 warp loops to stretch on the loom and 18 weft loops to weave over and under the warp.

2 Stretch the warp loops across the loom. Put one loop on every pair of pegs.

warp loops

Tip
If you run out of pegs on one side but not the other, you've skipped a peg somewhere. Find the place and adjust the loops.

3 Take your first weft loop and begin to weave it over and under the warp loops. Go OVER both strands of the first warp loop and UNDER both strands of the second loop.

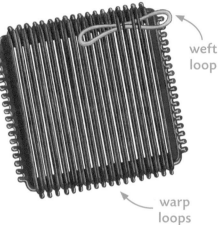

weft loop

warp loops

4 Keep weaving the weft loop over or under both strands of each warp loop.

5 Pull the front end of the loop toward the far side of the loom, and catch the tail end on the peg.

Catch here.

Pull here.

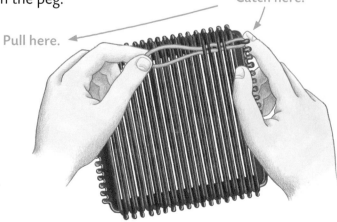

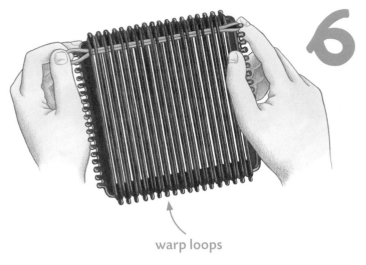

warp loops

6 Keep on weaving until you have gone under the very last warp loop.

Hook here.

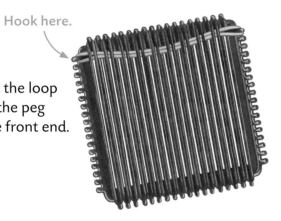

7 Hook the loop over the peg at the front end.

8 Use your hand like a rake to straighten the weft loop across the loom.

9 IMPORTANT: Start to weave in the second weft loop differently from the first. Go UNDER the first warp loop this time, OVER the second warp loop, and so on.

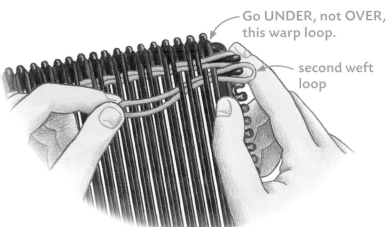

Go UNDER, not OVER, this warp loop.

second weft loop

10 Continue weaving the rest of the weft loops. Remember to switch back and forth as you begin each row: if you go over the first warp loop in one row, go UNDER the first loop in the next row.

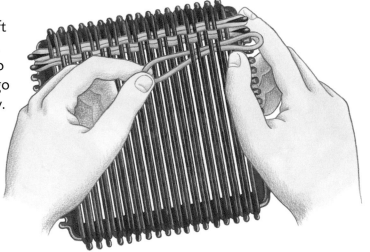

11 Every row or two, use your hand as a rake to straighten the weaving.

under-over under-over-under

12 If the last few loops are hard to weave, use your crochet hook to catch and pull them through.

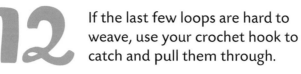

crochet hook

13 Leave your potholder on the loom until you finish the edges. Use woven edging (page 10) or loopy edging (page 26).

Once the edges are finished, you've got yourself a potholder. Keep it handy for all your potholding needs or, better yet, give it as a gift.

Many cooks think woven potholders are the best kind around, but they can't buy them in stores — they have to know someone with a loom who will weave some for them.

Warp loops go in
first, then weft —
it's alphabetical!

Woven Edging

This is the easiest way to finish off a potholder.

you will need:
- A square that you've finished weaving, still on the loom
- A crochet hook

1 Holding the loom so that one corner is pointing away from you, find the top loop on the right-hand side. This is loop 1.

loop 1

2 Catch loop 1 with your crochet hook and pull it off its peg.

loop 2

3 With loop 1 still on the crochet hook, poke the hook through the top loop on the left-hand side of the loom, and pull it off its peg. This is loop 2.

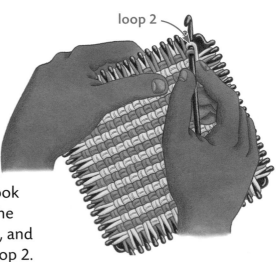

4 Lift loop 1 with your fingers. Use the hook to pull loop 2 through loop 1. Now you have only one loop on your hook again — loop 2.

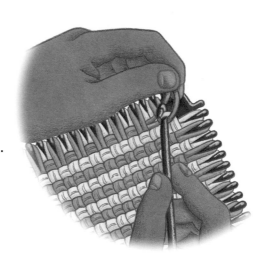

loop 3

5 With that loop still on the hook, poke the hook through the next loop to the left, and pull it off its peg. This is loop 3.

6 Repeat step 4, lifting loop 2 with your fingers, and pulling loop 3 through it using the hook. Once again you have only one loop on your hook.

7 Keep going along like this, always moving to the left. Be careful to keep the loops ahead of you on their pegs! When you come to a corner, just weave right around it the same way.

Work in this direction.

8 Once you have gone around the first two sides, one corner will be completely loose from the loom. Stretch the loose corner back and catch a loop from the edging on a corner peg. This will keep the weaving on the loom until you finish the edging.

Catch the next corner, too, once it's free.

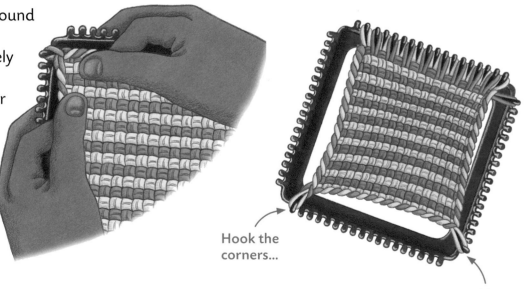

Hook the corners...

...so things stay organized.

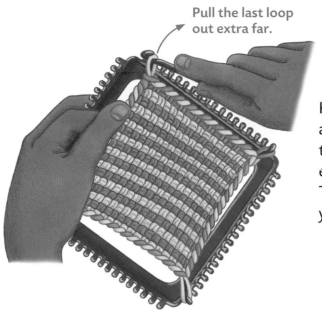

Pull the last loop
out extra far.

9

Keep weaving the edge all the way around the square until you come to the very last loop. Pull this loop extra far, so it won't pop back out. That loop will make it easy to hang your finished potholder on a peg.

10

Take your potholder off the loom and pull it this way and that to work it back into a square shape. That's it! A finished potholder that can be machine-washed and dried.

Done!

Turn a potholder into a Picture Frame

you will need:

- A potholder
- A photo
- 2 slender twigs, 5 1/2 inches (14 cm) long
- Yarn, 15 inches (38 cm) long
- Crochet hook

1 Center your photo on the potholder and lay the twigs over it as shown.

2 Find the four loops in the weaving that are right beneath the twigs and beside the photo. We've outlined them in blue here.

3 Use your crochet hook to pull the four loops up and stretch them.

4 Slip the twigs through the stretched loops.

5 Tie a piece of yarn to the top corners to make a picture hanger and slip the photo into its place behind the twigs.

Weaving Patterns

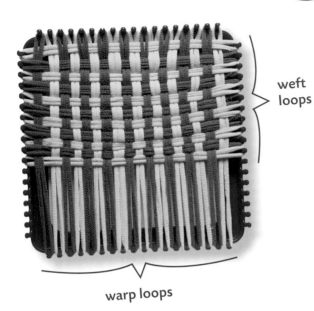

weft loops

warp loops

By arranging your warp and weft loops in a particular order, you can create a pattern as you weave. Just weave over and under as usual.

Stripes
2 colors

This one's super easy — just alternate between pink and green loops.

1

Follow this part of the pattern to arrange your warp loops on the loom. Each dot in this row shows the color for one warp loop.

2

Then weave the weft loops in the order shown here. Each dot in this row shows the color for one weft loop.

Pinwheel
2 colors

Just one tiny difference changes the Stripes pattern on page 16 into the Pinwheel pattern.

You can use your choice of colors in any of the patterns.

2 ⌐

Colors alternate except for the two in the middle.

2 ⌐

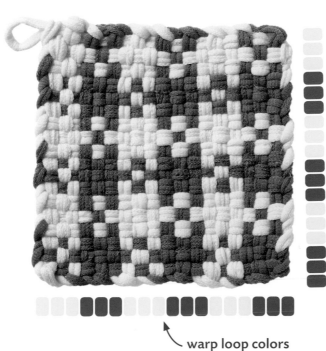

weft loop colors

Puzzle Pieces
2 colors

This potholder is made by using three of the first color, then three of the second color, then back to three of the first color again, and so on.

warp loop colors

Woven purse

you will need:
- 2 potholders finished with woven edges (page 10)
- 1 yard (about 1 meter) of yarn
- Plastic needle
- 10–14 extra loops for the strap

how to make the bag

1 Lay one square on top of the other with the end loops placed as shown.

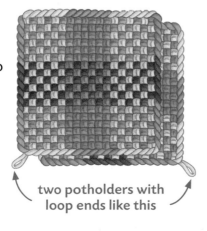

two potholders with loop ends like this

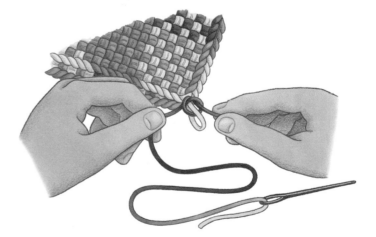

2 Tie one end of the yarn at the base of one of the end loops. Thread the needle with the other end.

3 Beginning at the base of the loop, sew the squares together. Poke the needle through both squares, pull it through, and then start another stitch right next to the spot where the needle first went in.

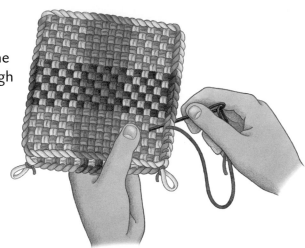

4 Sew down one side, across the bottom, and up the other side to the other end loop. Leave the top open.

Remove the needle and tie the yarn at the base of the loop.

open top

Tie knot here.

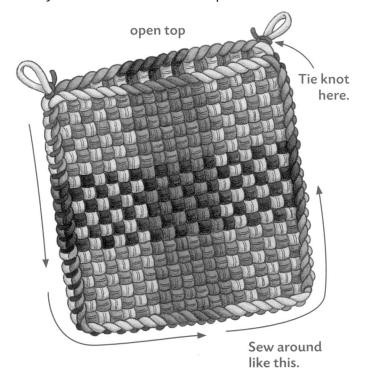

Sew around like this.

How to make the strap

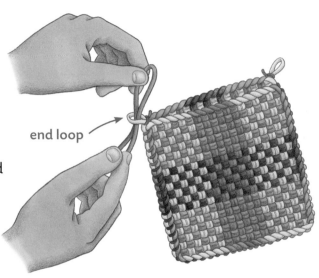

end loop

5 Put a loop through one of the end loops on the purse, taking one end of the loop with each hand.

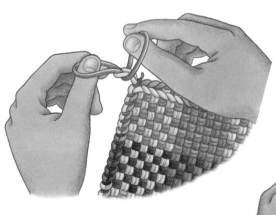

Swap the loop ends from one hand...

6 Pass the loop ends from hand-to-hand four or five times. Always pass the loop you find in your right hand through the loop you find in your left hand.

...to the other, 4 or 5 times.

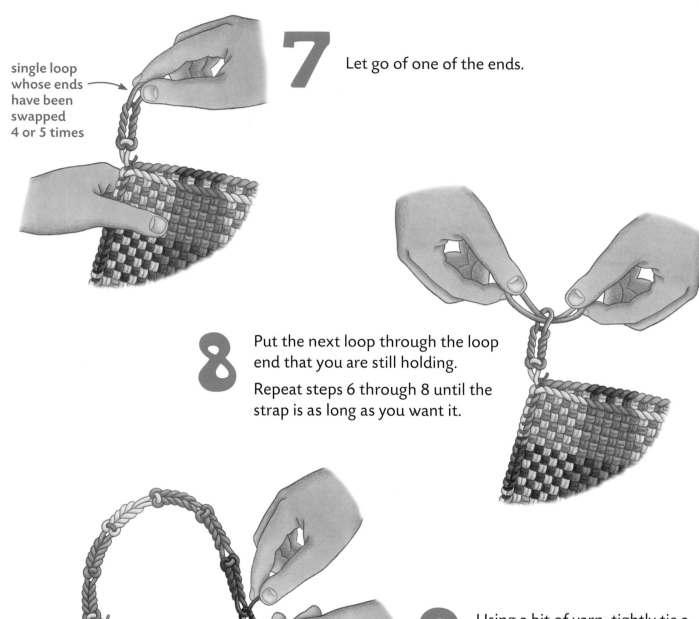

single loop
whose ends
have been
swapped
4 or 5 times

7 Let go of one of the ends.

8 Put the next loop through the loop end that you are still holding.

Repeat steps 6 through 8 until the strap is as long as you want it.

9 Using a bit of yarn, tightly tie a double knot fastening the last loop of the strap to the other end loop on the purse.

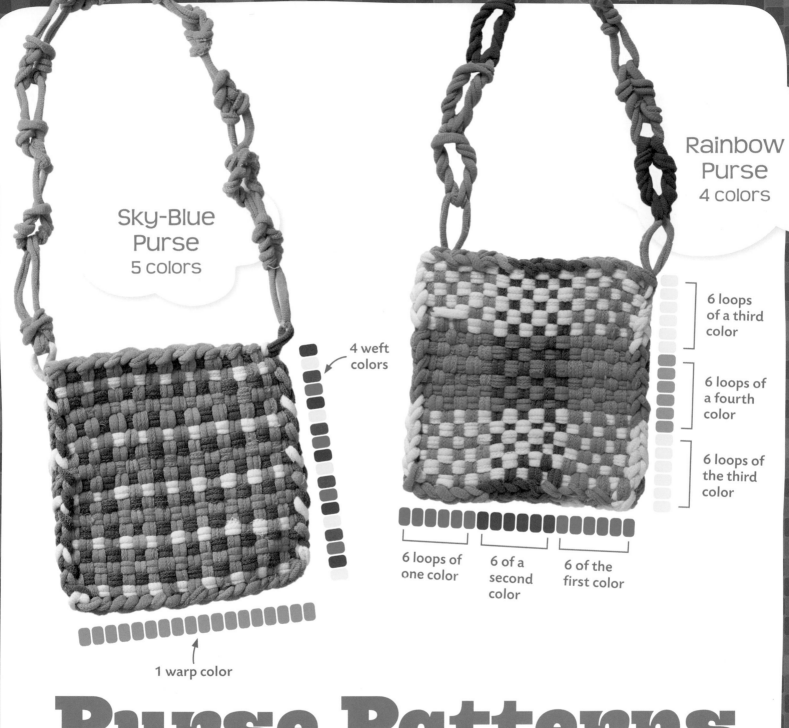

Sky-Blue Purse
5 colors

Rainbow Purse
4 colors

4 weft colors

1 warp color

6 loops of a third color

6 loops of a fourth color

6 loops of the third color

6 loops of one color

6 of a second color

6 of the first color

Purse Patterns

Tic-Tac-Toe

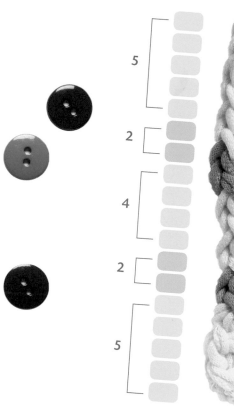

5
2
4
2
5

5 2 4 5 5

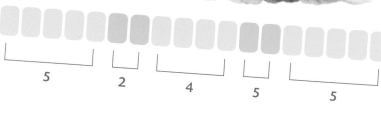

2 colors

Buttons make great playing pieces.

Checkers, Anyone?

16

16

3 colors

To get the checkerboard pattern, weave the blue loops, **two at a time**, over and under **pairs** of the red loops.

Loopy Edging

This is the second way to finish a potholder. The first is woven edging (page 10). If you're making a project that needs two squares linked together, this is the edging you'll have to have.

you will need:
- A woven square, still on the loom
- 2 1/2 yards (about 2.3 meters) of yarn
- A crochet hook

1 Fold one end of the yarn over 3–4 inches (8–10 cm) to make a loop.

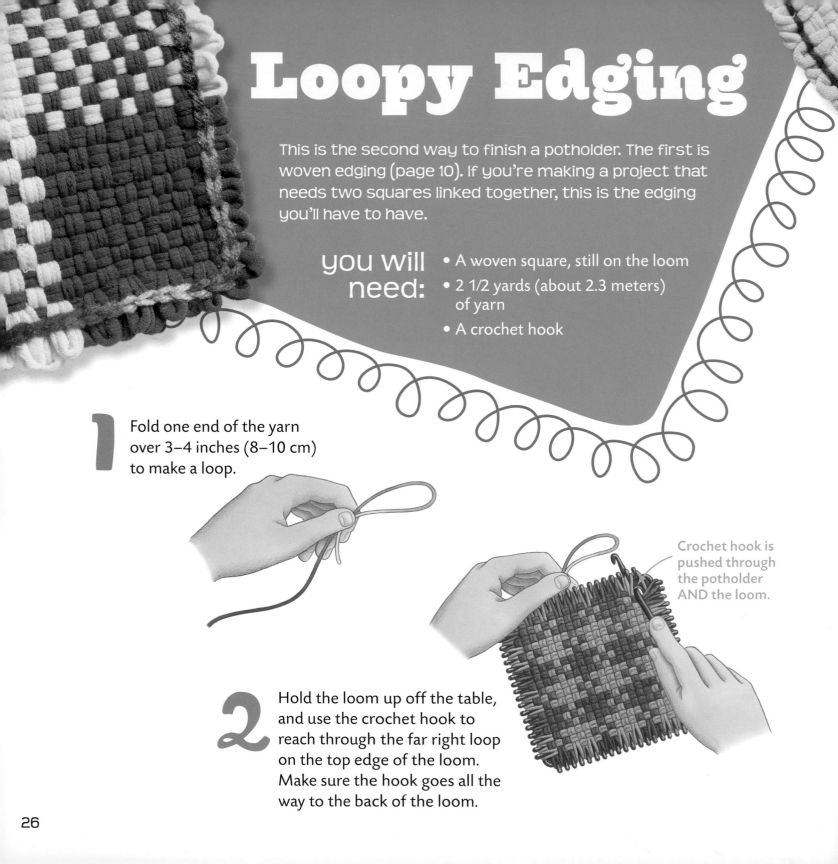

Crochet hook is pushed through the potholder AND the loom.

2 Hold the loom up off the table, and use the crochet hook to reach through the far right loop on the top edge of the loom. Make sure the hook goes all the way to the back of the loom.

3 Catch the yarn loop on the crochet hook. This is yarn loop 1.

yarn loop 1

4 Pull yarn loop 1 through the loom and the potholder loop.

That's going to be yarn loop 2.

5 With yarn loop 1 still on the hook, push the hook down through the next potholder loop to catch the long length of yarn from behind the loom. Be careful not to hook the short length of the yarn — let it fall to the right, out of the way.

6 Pull yarn loop 2 back through the potholder loop.

7 Making sure yarn loop 2 is right under the hook, turn the hook face down, and pull yarn loop 2 through yarn loop 1. Turn the hook face up after yarn loop 1 slips off the crochet hook. You will now have just one yarn loop on your crochet hook.

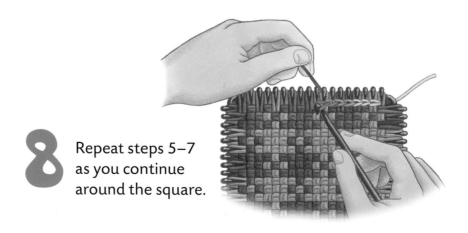

8 Repeat steps 5–7 as you continue around the square.

9 When you come back to the first potholder loop, pull a yarn loop through it in the usual way. Keeping the hook in place, trim the length of yarn from the back of the loom, and then pull it all the way through to the front of the loom

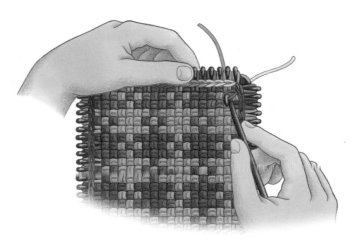

10 Slip the crochet hook under your very first stitch. Pull the short length of yarn to the front of the loom.

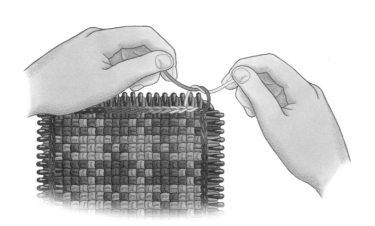

11 Tie the two loose ends in a double knot and trim to 1/4 inch (0.6 cm).

Done!

Big Beanbag

you will need:

- 2 potholders finished with loopy edges
- 6 inches (15.2 cm) of yarn
- Crochet hook
- Yarn needle
- 1 pound (0.5 kg) dried lima or kidney beans

1 Lay the two squares on top of each other.

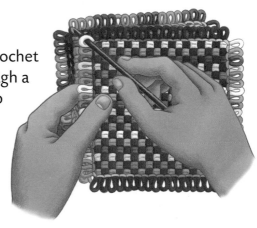

2 Push the crochet hook through a corner loop on the top square.

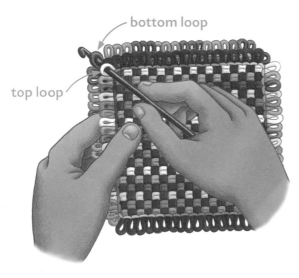

bottom loop

top loop

3 Then push the crochet hook through the same loop on the bottom square.

Top loop is now on bottom and off the hook.

Bottom loop is now on top.

 Pull the bottom loop through the top loop. The top loop comes off the hook.

Put the hook through this next loop.

This loop was already on the hook.

5 Now put the crochet hook through the next loop on the top square . . .

. . . and pull it through the loop already on the crochet hook, so there is only one loop left on the hook.

Let this loop slip off the hook.

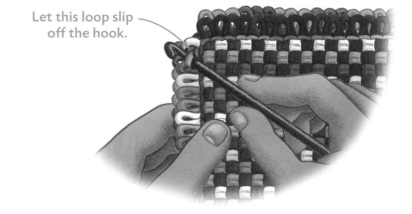

6 Go all the way around three sides, linking loops from the upper and lower squares.

7 When you come to the end of the third side, fill the bag with the dried beans.

Leave crochet hook in place.

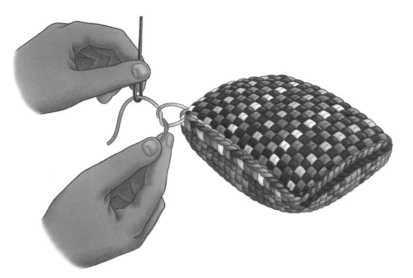

8

Close your beanbag by linking the last side until you have just one loop left. Poke the loop inside the beanbag and sew it in place using yarn and the yarn needle.

Instead of linking the squares together you could sew them together, as shown in the woven purse instructions on page 19.

More Weaving Patterns

9

9

9   9

Classic
2 colors

Nine loops of one color, followed by nine loops of a second color

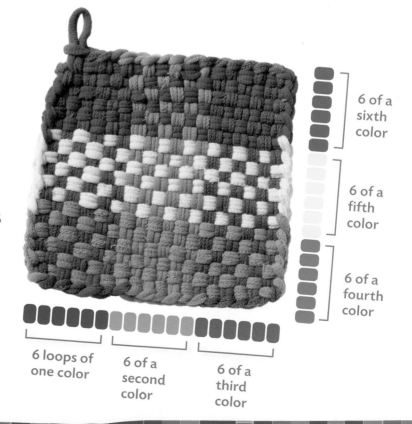

Fiesta
6 colors

6 of a sixth color

6 of a fifth color

6 of a fourth color

6 loops of one color

6 of a second color

6 of a third color

Hound's Tooth
2 colors

Two loops of one color followed by two loops of a second color, repeat

weft colors

warp colors

Weft loops are all one color.

Confetti
6 colors

5 warp colors take turns.

Loopy Chicken

1 Fold a potholder into a triangle. Starting at one end, weave the edges together as shown in the Beanbag instructions on page 30.

2 Keep weaving until you reach the point of the triangle. Stuff the potholder with cotton balls and then weave the remaining open edges together. At the end, close as in step 8 on page 33.

Comb, Wattle & Eye

Use the multi-colored yarn to sew on these features.

comb

wattle

3 Thread the needle with the mostly red yarn. Make a knot at the end that is the most reddish.

knot

4 Now you'll sew loopy stitches to make the comb and wattle.

Start with a small tight stitch, then make a long loopy stitch that you leave loose. Next make another small tight stitch. Go back and forth between loopy and tight stitches and make a knot at the end.

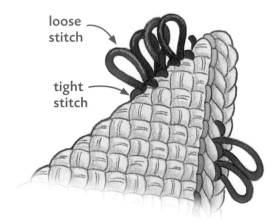

loose stitch

tight stitch

5 Thread the needle with the mostly blue yarn and make a knot at one end.

knot

6 Sew a few stitches on each side of the head to make the eyes. Make a knot when finished.

Tail Feathers

7 For the tail, use your crochet hook to pull each loop halfway through the weaving as shown. Play around with the tail until you like the way it looks. Eggcellent.

EDITOR
Karen Phillips

DESIGNER
Keeli McCarthy

LOOP WRANGLERS
Kelly Beltramo
Patty Morris

PACKAGE DESIGNER
David Avidor

PRODUCTION EDITOR
Madeleine Robins

ILLUSTRATOR
Barbara Ball

PHOTOGRAPHERS
Matthew Farruggio
Peter Fox
Joseph Quever

LOOPY IDEAS
Alice Tucker

TRUE BEWEAVER
Rebekah Lovato

HOT STUFF
Jill Turney

MODELS
Marcos Amaral
Sonali Kumar
Lauren McGary
Searah R. Norman
Julie Persson
Jenae-Ann E. Robinson
Atom Rognuson
Lily Seedman
Madeline Siu

Here are more Klutz books
we think your kids will like.

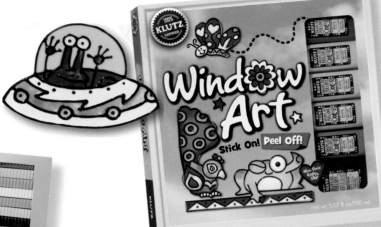